DATE DUE

1998	

PRINTED IN U.S.A.

The United States

California

Anne Welsbacher
ABDO & Daughters

visit us at
www.abdopub.com

Published by Abdo & Daughters, 4940 Viking Drive, Suite 622, Edina, Minnesota 55435. Copyright © 1998 by Abdo Consulting Group, Inc., Pentagon Tower, P.O. Box 36036, Minneapolis, Minnesota 55435 USA. International copyrights reserved in all countries. No part of this book may be reproduced in any form without written permission from the publisher.

Printed in the United States.

Cover and Interior Photo credits: Peter Arnold, Inc., Super Stock , Archive Photos

Edited by Lori Kinstad Pupeza
Contributing editor Brooke Henderson
Special thanks to our Checkerboard Kids—Raymond Sherman, Shane Wagner, Peter Rengstorf, Francesca Tuminelly

All statistics taken from the 1990 census; The Rand McNally Discovery Atlas of The United States. Other sources: America Online, Compton's Living Encyclopedia, 1997; World Book Encyclopedia, 1990.

Library of Congress Cataloging-in-Publication Data

Welsbacher, Anne, 1955-
    California / Anne Welsbacher.
    p. cm. -- (United States)
    Includes index.
    Summary: Surveys the people, geography, and history of the western state that has more people than any other state.
    ISBN 1-56239-862-8
    1. California--Juvenile literature. [1. California.] I. Title. II. Series: United States (Series)
F861.3.W45   1998   97-8506
979.4--dc21   CIP
                                       AC

Contents

Welcome to California

California is number one in many ways. It has more people and farmland than any other state.

Even long ago, California had many people. As many as 500 Native American nations lived in California. Today, most of those nations are gone. Now, people from all around the world live in California.

California has mountains, deserts, and forests. It has beaches, too. In most of California it is sunny and warm all year long. That is why so many people live there.

Opposite page: Big Sur Coast, California.

Fast Facts

CALIFORNIA

Capital
Sacramento (369,365 people)
Area
156,297 square miles
(404,807 sq km)
Population
29,839,250 people
Rank: 1st
Statehood
Sept. 9, 1850
(31st state admitted)
Principal rivers
Colorado River,
Sacramento River,
San Joaquin River
Highest point
Mount Whitney; 14,494 feet
(4,418 m)
Largest City
Los Angeles (3,485,398 people)
Motto
Eureka
(I have found it)
Song
"I Love You California"
Famous People
Shirley Temple Black, Cesar
Chavez, William Randolph
Hearst, Marilyn Monroe, Ronald
Reagan, Sally Ride

*S*tate Flag

*G*olden Poppy

*C*alifornia Valley
Quail

*C*alifornia Redwood

About California

The Golden State

Detail area

California's abbreviation

Borders: west (Pacific Ocean), north (Oregon), east (Nevada, Arizona), south (Mexico)

Nature's Treasures

California is called the Golden State. In the 1800s, much gold was mined out of California's land. Later, oil was found. Oil is sometimes called **black gold**.

California has many forests. So timber is another treasure from California. Timber is wood made from trees that are cut down.

Almost half of California is farmland. Its rich soils come from river valleys. California soils have many minerals, as well.

The weather is a real treasure in California. In some parts of California it is sunny and warm all year long. Many people visit California to enjoy its weather.

The sun going down over California grape vines.

Beginnings

The first Californians lived almost 12,000 years ago. Between 100 and 500 groups of Native Americans lived in California. Some Native Americans fished. Others hunted. Still others farmed. These groups of people were named Shasta, Pomo, Miwok, Chumash, Mojave, and Yokut.

In the 1500s, Spanish explorers **claimed** California and built **missions**. The Spanish spread their diseases to the Native Americans. Many Native Americans died from the diseases. In 1821 Mexico won a war with Spain. Then Mexico owned California.

In 1848 the United States won a war with Mexico. California then became a part of the United States. Also in 1848, gold was found in California. Within a year, many people came to California to dig for gold. This was called the **gold rush**.

In 1850, California became the 31st state to join the United States. In 1869 a long railroad was built across the United States. Then even more people could come to California!

In the 1900s, the movies were **invented**. Many movies were filmed in California. People came to California to work in the film **industry**. People also came to California to farm.

In 1906 a great earthquake shook the city of San Francisco. Even today there are many earthquakes in California. But people still come to California! In 1963 California became the state with the most people.

Gold miner in California, 1852.

11

B.C. to 1700s

The First Californians

12,000-10,000 B.C.: The first Native Americans move to the land now called California. Later other nations live all through the area. Between 100 and 500 groups of Native Americans live as separate cultures.

1542: Juan Rodriquez Cabrillo is the first person from Europe who visits California. He is from Spain.

1769: The first **mission** is built in San Diego, California.

California

B.C. to 1700s

1800s

Golden Times

1849: The **gold rush** begins. Miners are called 49ers because of the year they arrive in California.

1850: California becomes the 31st state.

1869: Around 10,000 Chinese workers help build parts of a railroad that stretches across the country to California.

California

1800s

1911 to Today

The 20th Century

 1911: The first movie is made in Hollywood, California.

 1968: Redwood National Park opens.

 1973: Tom Bradley becomes the first African-American mayor of Los Angeles.

 1989: A big earthquake hits northern California.

California

1911 to Today

California's People

There are almost 30 million people in California. That is like 10 Colorados full of people! Almost everybody lives in a city.

Today's Californians are from everywhere! They are from Mexico, China, and Japan. They are from the Philippines, Vietnam, and South Korea.

More Mexican people live in the city of Los Angeles than in any other city outside of Mexico.

Californians are African American, Latino, Asian, Native American, and white. Latino people came from Central America and South America.

Cesar Chavez came from California. He founded the United Farm Workers of America. Baseball great Joe DiMaggio is from California. And astronaut Sally Ride is from California.

Two well loved writers from California were John Steinbeck and Jack London. Former President Richard Nixon also was from California. And Steven Jobs and Steven Wozniak, who started the Apple Computer company, are from California.

Movie stars Tom Hanks, Cher, Shirley Temple, and Marilyn Monroe were born in California. So was the man who **invented** Mickey Mouse: Walt Disney!

John Steinbeck

Marilyn Monroe

Walt Disney

Splendid Cities

Los Angeles is the largest city in California. It has the most people and the most land. It is in southern California. San Diego is also in southern California. Pretty beaches border the Pacific Ocean. It is almost always sunny and warm in San Diego.

San Francisco is in northern California. It is near the ocean. It has many pretty bridges. It has many hills.

Los Angeles and San Francisco both have an area called Chinatown. Many Chinese people live in Chinatown.

Sacramento

San Francisco

San Jose

Los Angeles

San Diego

San Francisco, San Jose, and Sacramento are all in northern California. Sacramento is the capital of California.

The city of Los Angeles, California.

CALIFORNIA REPUBLIC

California's Land

California is shaped like a banana. It stretches all the way from Oregon to Mexico! To the east are the states of Nevada and Arizona. To the west is the Pacific Ocean.

California has four different types of land. Mountains stand next to the ocean. The central valley lies east of the mountains. This is good farmland.

East of the valley is another mountain area. Mount Whitney is in this area.

The great **basin** lies in the east part of California. There are deserts in this basin. One desert is very dry and hot. It is called Death Valley.

Northern California's forests are filled with giant trees. Some of these are the oldest trees in the world. And some are the largest in the world, too. It would take eight of your friends to reach all the way around the biggest of them! These trees are called sequoia and redwood.

There are about 8,000 lakes in California. Lake Tahoe is the deepest lake in California. Ribbon Falls is the highest waterfall in North America!

Pretty wild flowers grow in northern California and cactuses grow in the desert.

Beavers, bears, and wildcats live in California. Wildlife refuges are home to pelicans, peregrine falcons, and hundreds of other birds.

California has two seasons: rainy and dry. It snows and can be cold in northern California. But it is warm all year long in southern California!

Death Valley in California.

California at Play

Disneyland is a huge playground in southern California. It has a giant castle and many rides. It is the home of Mickey Mouse and many other Disney friends.

The San Diego Zoo is one of the world's largest zoos. Eight hundred animals live there! Sea World is also in San Diego. There you can watch sea creatures like dolphins play in the water.

California has many **scenic** parks. They are in mountains, in forests, and near beaches. You can fish, sit in the sun, ride horseback, camp, hike, or scuba-dive. The Redwood Highway goes through the tall redwood forests. On one road, cars can drive right through a trunk of a giant redwood tree!

There are five baseball teams in California. They are the San Francisco Giants, the Oakland A's, the Los Angeles Dodgers, the San Diego Padres, and the Anaheim

Angels. California football teams include the Oakland Raiders, the San Francisco 49ers, and the San Diego Chargers. The Rose Bowl football game is played in Pasadena, California.

In San Francisco is Fisherman's Wharf. You can buy fish there or take a boat trip in the **bay**.

The dolphin show at Sea World.

California at Work

The movies are big business in California! Besides working in the movies, people also work in radio, music, and TV.

Many people work in **manufacturing** or work with computers. The Apple Computer company is in California. Many other computer companies also are in California.

Lots of farmers work in California. More than half of the fruits and nuts in the whole country are grown in California! California **produces** cotton and wheat, and raises cows. Grapes are grown and sold fresh. They also are made into raisins, grape juice, and wine.

A lot of people work in service. Service is cooking and serving food, working in parks like Disneyland, and doing other things for **tourists** who visit the state.

Some Californians fish. They catch shrimp, tuna, and other fish. Others build ships. Others are **loggers**. They cut trees to make into paper and other things.

The Apple Computer Building in California.

Fun Facts

•Many rare animals and plants live in California. They include the blue whale, the bald eagle, and the San Francisco popcorn flower.

•The highest mountain in the continental United States is Mount Whitney in California. It is 14,494 feet (4,418 meters).

•California is the third biggest state in the United States. It is 156,297 square miles (404,807 sq km).

•California's nickname is the Golden State. This is partly because miners dug so much gold out of California. But the name also is for the golden dreams that people have when they move to California.

•Four cities in California are on the list of the 20 biggest cities in the whole country. They are Los Angeles, San Francisco, San Diego, and San Jose.

•There are real castles in California. One is called the Hearst Castle at San Simeon. It was designed by Julia Morgan. She designed 700 buildings!

•Parts of California use windmills to make energy. California's state motto is "Eureka." That means "I have found it."

•Alcatraz is an island near San Francisco. A prison was built on the island, but it is not used anymore. No one ever escaped alive from Alcatraz.

•Food is fun in California! The state has a garlic festival, a clam-digging contest, and even a party for asparagus!

•There are about 200 parks and playgrounds in Los Angeles.

Alcatraz Island near San Francisco.

Glossary

Bay: an area of the ocean near the land.

Basin: the land that is drained by a river and the streams that flow into the river.

Black gold: a nickname for oil.

Claim: to take, or call your own.

Continental: the 48 states on the mainland, not including Hawaii and Alaska.

Gold rush-1849: the time when many miners came to California to dig for gold.

Industry: any type of business.

Invent: to make for the first time.

Logger: a person who cuts down trees to make into paper and other things.

Manufacture: to make things.

Mission: a large church or group of buildings.

Produce: to make something.

Reservation: land set aside for Native Americans.

Scenic: having to do with natural scenery, or the outdoors.

Timberwood: wood made from trees that have been cut down.

Tourist: a person who travels for fun.

Internet Sites

California Online
http://californiaonline.com
We are your one stop place for "what's hot" in your area. Here you will find something of interest for everybody. Shopping, restaurants, hotels, travel, entertainment, medical services, legal services, auto repair, hairdressers, you name it.

Coolspots California
http://www.coolspots.com
CoolSpots has thousands of photographs and some text of national, state, and local historical landmarks, along with historic structures and funky sites, mainly in California.

These sites are subject to change. Go to your favorite search engine and type in California for more sites.

PASS IT ON

Tell Others Something Special About Your State

To educate readers around the country, pass on interesting tips, places to see, history, and little unknown facts about the state you live in. We want to hear from you!

To get posted on ABDO & Daughters website E-mail us at "mystate@abdopub.com"

Index

C—
976.7
Wy

Welsbacher
Arkansas
32654

DATE DUE

1998

PRINTED IN U.S.A.